D0624531

JUST ADD WATER®

T1-AYN-995

Copyright © 2015 by Michael Baldwin.
All rights reserved.

Written by Michael Baldwin.

Edited by Catherine Johnson and Emma McLaughlin.

Design by Marc Klein.

Although every precaution has been taken to verify the accuracy of the information contained herein, the author and publisher assume no responsibility for any errors or omissions. No liability is assumed for damages that may result from the use of information contained within.

Published by Inkshares, Inc., San Francisco, California.

Printed in China.

Second Edition.

2 3 4 5 6 7 8 9 10

Library of Congress Control Number: 2015933217

ISBN 978-1-941758-28-1
(Paperback)

MICHAEL BALDWIN

JUST ADD WATER®

INKSHARES

SAN FRANCISCO

FOREWORD

I have spent 25 years in advertising, trained as a professional actor, delivered nearly 1,000 theater workshops at the flagship Apple Store, and made branding and marketing presentations powerful enough to convince even Steve Jobs. For the past five years, I've dedicated myself to helping senior managers, VPs, CMOs, and CEOs become better presenters.

I love the art of presentation. And I hate what's become of it. We were off to such a spectacular start 32,000 years ago with the simple, powerful cave paintings: the gold standard for presentations. Even Picasso was moved by their uncomplicated beauty and ability to communicate. But we've been in a downward spiral ever since. I'm all too aware of the drill: a mandate comes down from on high or from a client, a scramble ensues for all the relevant data, and everyone and their sister have to add their two cents before signing off. The result is a schizophrenic, overloaded presentation that nobody is happy with. Too many people spend weeks preparing a presentation only to see it tank, and don't know why or where to turn for help.

I've worked with six clients a day over the past five years and witnessed the frustration, confusion, and fear that so many people have about public speaking. I've seen these same clients transformed over the course of my training—and the joy and empowerment they feel as a result. This book is a distillation of that one-day program—and it works.

Here I turn the fundamentals of creating, organizing, and delivering content into easy-to-remember concepts. *Just Add Water* is shorthand for "easy." In the time it takes to fly from New York to Denver, it will give you the techniques to save time and energy in your preparation process and provide you a visual overview of what effective presentations look like. You'll discover how to create simple, powerful presentations that work.

"Nothing will accelerate your career faster than developing your ability to communicate."
—Stand and Deliver

ACKNOWLEDGMENTS

This book would not have been possible without the talent and tenacity of its designer, Marc Klein. I would like to thank him for creating such a beautiful and unexpected aesthetic and for introducing me to the other key contributors to the book: Catherine Johnson—photography and visuals; Emma McLaughlin—editor; and Vikram Patel—print designer. I am grateful to each of them for devoting their time and energy to this mission.

I would also like to thank my siblings—David, Jennifer, and Susannah—for being invaluable sounding boards and contributors and Reyn Parsons for his unflagging support and for getting me over the crowd-funding finish line.

Finally, I would like to thank all the clients I've had the pleasure of working with over the past eight years. It is the collective learning from every one of those engagements that has made this book possible.

Thank you.

POWERPOINT IS A
POWERFUL TOOL,
BUT PEOPLE NEED TO
LEARN HOW TO USE IT.
EVEN HARRY POTTER
HAD TO LEARN HOW
TO HARNESS THE
POWER OF HIS WAND.

JUST ADD WATER

DRIVING YOUR AUDIENCE FROM POINT "A" TO POINT "B"

A presentation is your opportunity to transport an audience from point "A" — their point of view on the subject when they come into the room — to point "B," where you want them to be on the subject when they leave.

From resistant to supportive.

From indifferent to committed.

From uninformed to educated.

To do this you'll need to know where they are and where you want to take them:

> Audience Perspective (where they are).

> Crystal Clear Objective (where you want to take them).

These seem like simple concepts, but don't be fooled. They're no less than the foundation of every presentation, and they require some thought and often a little research to determine. The majority of presentations that fail do so because the presenter didn't have these two elements established.

Any presentation is merely an opportunity to transport an audience from where they are to where you want them to be.

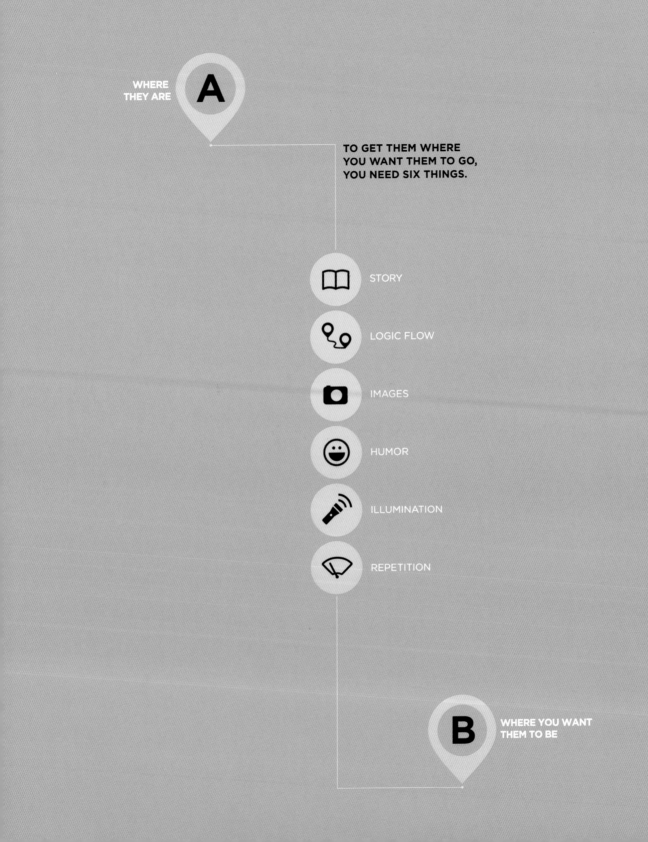

WHERE
THEY ARE

A

TO GET THEM WHERE
YOU WANT THEM TO GO,
YOU NEED SIX THINGS.

STORY

LOGIC FLOW

IMAGES

HUMOR

ILLUMINATION

REPETITION

B

WHERE YOU WANT
THEM TO BE

KNOW WHAT
YOUR AUDIENCE
IS THINKING—OR
PAY THE PRICE FOR
MAKING UNINFORMED
ASSUMPTIONS.

Your audience's point of view on the subject when they come into the room, including their biases and sensibilities, is your starting point. Would you tell the same joke to a room filled with investment bankers as you would to punk rockers? Probably not. Because they are two different groups of people, with different life experiences, concerns, and expectations. As a speaker, your job is to know as much as you possibly can about the people you will face. Specifically:

> What is their point of view, bias, and disposition regarding your presentation?
>
> How will your presentation potentially impact what they have at stake?
>
> What questions/issues might they have regarding your presentation?

The more you know about your audience and their predispositions, the better your chances of transporting them. This knowledge also equips you to anticipate questions or resistance so you can defuse responses that could derail you midstream.

EXERCISE

Write down at least one word that accurately describes your audience's state of mind regarding your presentation. Are they skeptical, exhausted, ignorant, sympathetic, or are they hostile?

Would you tell the same joke to investment bankers as you would to punk rockers? Why not?

*Almost all executives
I've worked with
have had a hard time
expressing their
Crystal Clear Objective
in one simple phrase.*

So, what makes an objective crystal clear? The fact that it can
be expressed in one simple phrase. It begins with the word "to."
The next word is the single-minded objective of every actor

poke
tease
calm flirt scold cc
ridicule pacify
console plead hu
comfort enrag
mastermind convince
ple
woo reprimar
appease rep
shock ignore kow
threaten command
hedge c
crucify enliven pa a

in stage, film, and television. It's the word that film critics use to unequivocally affirm a brilliant performance. Can you find it in the list of what actors call "action verbs" below?

rture evade interrogate
ce exasperate frighten
thral idolize lecture
or push hypnotize
astonish distract dodge
toy corner seduce
e challenge cajole
se beg bribe accuse
w urge pull shock fun
patronize confront
bute charm
per berate question
use defend adore

So the first two words in a Crystal Clear Objective (CCO) are "to convince."

Now it's up to you to finish the phrase for your own CCO:

to convince [*my audience*] that [*my main point*]

Here are a few examples:

> to convince faculty that Saturday classes will raise test scores

> to convince journalists that today's news business is volatile

> to convince my wife that I deserve a motorcycle

Almost all executives I've worked with find this challenging, even when they're attempting to craft it for a presentation they've already given many times.

Having a CCO when presenting to a CEO is critical. CEOs have no time to waste. They're listening for the single reason you're there. When that CEO is Steve Jobs—my client when he was at NeXT Computer—the clarity of my CCO is a matter of career life and death; the difference between Steve listening to my presentation or walking out of the room.

"Mr. Day-Lewis is startling, unsettling, and entirely convincing as Lincoln."
—A.O. Scott, the New York Times

CONVINCE

THE WORD
THAT FILM
CRITICS USE TO
ACKNOWLEDGE
A TRULY
REMARKABLE
ACHIEVEMENT
BY AN ACTOR.

A lack of focus on the presenter's part is obvious. It confuses the audience, creates frustration, and causes them to tune (or walk) out. And they don't tune back in. If you pretend that every person you present to is Steve Jobs, you won't risk wasting his or her time because you didn't do your homework

Boil your CCO down so it doesn't contain a single extra word, and build your presentation from there. It's your foundation. Everything in your presentation must serve your CCO. If it doesn't, *get rid of it.*

EXERCISE

Write down your CCO. Your goal is to have one simple phrase without buzzwords or jargon or a single extra word:

"to convince [*my audience*] that [*my main point*]"

If you aren't crystal clear about your objective within the first 90 seconds of a presentation to Steve Jobs, he might get up and walk out.

YOU ARE THE DRIVER, NOT YOUR SLIDES

You know what it's like to be at the mercy of your slides—that sickening moment when you realize everyone's glazing over and you're only halfway through the key points. You've been reduced to a narrator.

Don't let this happen. The relationship between you and your slides should always be:

You = Master

Your slides = Apprentice

Many presenters have this backward and as a result are marginalized in their audience's mind. Take the way we interpret a cartoon. We see the image, then read the caption, in that order. The caption deciphers the image. When presenting, you, the Master, should provide the caption. Without your explanation, your audience would have no clue what the cartoon on the left is about. With it, however, the meaning—and the humor—is unmistakable.

"Paper or plastic?"

YOU are whom the audience came to see.

YOU are the expert.

YOU should be the focus of any presentation you give.

YOU should offer the explanations, context, and references that make any slide you create make sense to an audience.

Your slides allow you to share images, video, graphs, and tables, which are there to serve and amplify YOU. They should never be the star.

START YOUR TRIP POWERFULLY: WITH A STORY

Even 32,000 years ago, the need to congregate and share was in our DNA. It remains there today, fueling the explosion of social media. Storytelling will always be part of our sharing process. If you're a parent, you see firsthand the pivotal role it plays in educating and entertaining your children, while creating a bond between you both. Stories have the power to plant situations, scenes, characters, and images in people's minds that they'll never forget.

There's no more effective way to engage an audience and capture its attention—right from the start—than with a story that communicates your CCO.

If you can come up with a personal story, you've hit the jackpot.

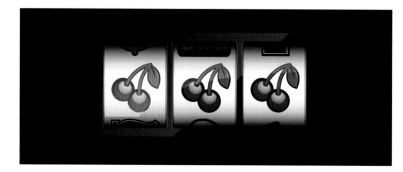

There are three elements to hitting the jackpot when it comes to story:

>   a CCO

>   a story that illustrates your CCO

>   a personal story

Personal storytelling can also eliminate hurdles presenters can face when they first start to speak:

>   nervousness

>   disconnection from their material

>   disconnection from their audience

Things I am
passionate about...

NO PREPARATION. NO REHEARSING.
NO NERVOUSNESS. EVERYONE CAN
TALK ABOUT HIS OR HER PASSIONS,
FROM ONE TO THE NEXT, RAPID-FIRE,
WITHOUT SKIPPING A BEAT.

You'd be amazed how these hurdles disappear when you're telling a personal story. Pick a memory—your first crush, your favorite vacation—and start talking about it. Do you feel the need to rehearse? Do you feel disconnected from the events you are recounting? Do you feel nervous?

No. Because you actually lived the experience. And when you talk about it—far from trying to make sure you get it right—you're connected with the players and emotions. And if you're like every single person I've worked with, you automatically become animated and engaging.

If you don't have a personal story that applies to your presentation, then subjects you're passionate about can be just as effective:

> You have direct experiences with them.
>
> You become animated when you talk about them.
>
> You can talk about them without hesitation or preparation.

Stories have the power to plant situations, scenes, characters, and images in people's minds that they'll never forget.

Subjects or activities you're passionate about accumulate over your life in what I call your "Passion Trunk." When the time comes to craft a story that communicates your CCO, look there first.

Here's an example of one of my clients in supply chain management at a global retail fashion company. His CCO: to convince his superiors that supply chain management was a critical factor to his company's success. One of his passions was World War II history. This was his story:

> In one of the last World War II battles in France, the US Sherman tanks were pitted against the German Panzer tanks. In every respect, the German Panzer tank was superior: there were more of them, they had better armor and they had longer-range guns. They had every advantage going in.

Your "Passion Trunk" is where all your memories of your favorite things are stored. Look inside it when you begin crafting your story.

At the end of the battle, the Germans were defeated, rather soundly, for one major reason: they ran out of fuel. Their supply chain let them down.

So while it is a huge advantage to have a great tank with great guns, and great armor that's more nimble in the battlefield—if you can't move, you'll lose the battle.

Our supply chain is much like the fuel: we need to make sure our product gets to the retail floor first—every time—so when a customer is in the store, whether it's our store or one of our customer's, that consumer can buy our product and take it home.

He illustrated his CCO for his audience—that the supply-chain is a "critical factor for success"—with an unforgettable WWII story about a supply-chain. Bravo.

An alternative is to look into your audience's "Collective Experience Trunk" to craft your story.

Another client is in healthcare administration. Rather than use a story from his personal experiences or passions, he looked into the collective experiences of his audience, who were doctors across the spectrum of healthcare, from neurology to clinical psychiatry.

Illustrating ease of implementation of a new system with a story about a previous installation. Bravo.

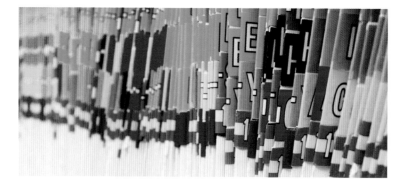

His CCO: to convince these doctors that the new patient processing system would be easy to implement across their departments. This was his story:

> Five years ago, a large medical institution decided to upgrade its billing system. The doctors were dead set against it, worried that it would be a nightmare to install a new system, train the staff, and learn a new interface.
>
> The doctors were overruled, and the new system was implemented. As it turned out, the installation process went smoothly, as did the training. Everyone preferred the new system. Which medical institution am I referring to?
>
> Ours.
>
> And which doctors am I referring to?
>
> You.
>
> Now, by show of hands, how many of you would like to go back to the old billing system? [Not one hand was raised.]
>
> So, why am I here today? To give you an overview of the new patient processing system we are preparing to implement. And to demonstrate how easy the implementation and training process

YOUR STORY SHOULD BE A
PERFECT ILLUSTRATION OF YOUR
CRYSTAL CLEAR OBJECTIVE.

THE JUSTICE ILLUSTRATED THE CRUX OF THE CASE WITH A SIMPLE 334-YEAR-OLD FABLE. AND IT WORKED PERFECTLY.

will be—as easy as it was for the billing system five years ago. And it will become just as invaluable to you.

My client looked into his audience's collective experience to effectively illustrate his CCO.

There are two other things to keep in mind when crafting your story.

CONCRETE VS. ABSTRACT

Stick to concepts that are simple and concrete. This is even more vital when presenting to a multicultural audience, where your story has to be understood by people with different backgrounds and worldviews.

In 2011 there was a famous lawsuit in which a supervisor convinced his company to discriminate against another employee. When the employee sued the company for discrimination, the company was found to be at fault, not the supervisor.

In his ruling, the supreme court justice used a fable from 1679, by La Fontaine, to illustrate the dynamics of the case. In the fable, a monkey convinces a cat to pull roasting chestnuts from the fire. After the cat has done so, the monkey eats the chestnuts and leaves the cat with nothing but burned paws. In the legal context, the monkey is the supervisor orchestrating the discrimination, and the employer is the cat, whose paws are burned due to the supervisor's actions.

There are any number of complex ways this judge could have attempted to illustrate the crux of the case. He chose a simple 334-year-old fable. And it worked perfectly.

In a recent discussion on *Meet the Press* about same-sex marriage, one advocate for legalization made a point about how unfair it is when married same-sex couples visit different states,

The best stories are simple, emotional, vivid, authentic, and personal.

of which some recognize their unions and some don't. He said: "The legal status of same-sex couples shouldn't vary from state to state like the signal strength on a cell phone."

Simple. Concrete. It means you can communicate immediately with no work required on the part of the audience. You don't need to explain the concept of burned paws or cell phone signal strength.

Idioms also communicate with any audience instantly:

"Rob Peter to pay Paul."

"A bird in the hand is worth two in the bush."

"Penny-wise, pound-foolish."

"The legal status of same-sex couples shouldn't vary like the signal strength on a cell phone." Simple, concrete, and no work required on the part of the audience to understand it immediately.

They have been around for thousands of years, across many cultures, and have the power to make a point immediately and universally.

MULTIPLE HOOKS CAN MAKE YOUR STORY UNFORGETTABLE

Keep in mind that human beings use more than just their sense of sound to experience stories. So why engage your audience using only your voice? Why not show them a video clip that they'll never forget? Or utilize a smell—pleasant or unpleasant—that will stick with them? Or hand out samples of a particular food to give them a taste of something they will always remember? Or ask them to close their eyes and listen to a piece of music? Or touch silk or sandpaper? I only have to remember my first "haunted house" to viscerally understand this phenomenon:

putting my hand in a bowl of human intestines (bowl of Jell-O)

smelling a witch's cauldron (smoky fire in metal barrel)

touching corpses hanging from the ceiling (Halloween masks)

SIGHT, SOUND, SMELL, TOUCH, TASTE.
HOW MANY OF THESE FIVE SENSES ARE
ENGAGED BY YOUR STORY?

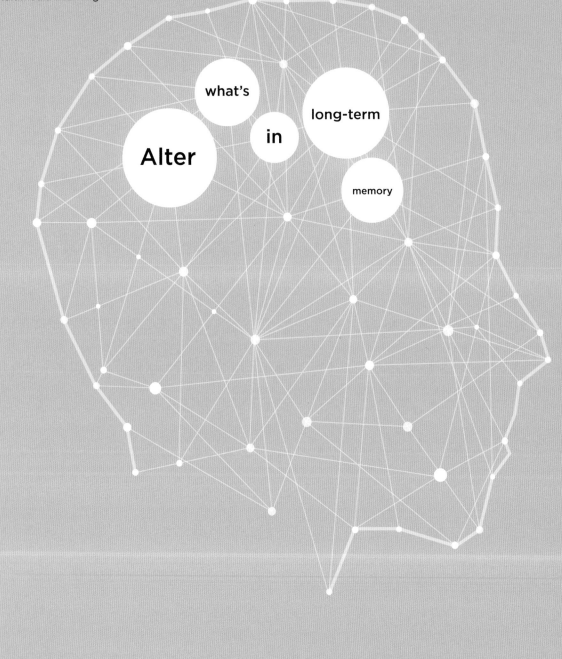

IF NOTHING HAS BEEN ALTERED IN LONG-TERM MEMORY, NOTHING HAS BEEN LEARNED.
—*Cambridge Handbook of Multimedia Learning*

Alter what's in long-term memory

I was in sixth grade. It was over 45 years ago. I walked through only once, but because the experience stimulated all my senses, it left an impression that I can conjure in detail even today. I can still remember holding what I was told were witches' eyeballs in my hand. Now that's an effective presentation!

What kind of experience can you come up with to support your CCO that your audience will still remember in 2058?

ALTERNATIVE ROUTES TO START YOUR TRIP

There are alternatives to telling a story when beginning your trip. Any of these could work:

> a provocative question

> a surprising fact or statistic

> an interesting quote

But a story is the most powerful way to illustrate your CCO and capture the imagination of your audience.

LEVERAGING LONG-TERM MEMORIES

Let's say I'm pitching a movie concept to a big studio. I could pitch it this way:

"It's about a young girl. She's not disabled but has trouble running. The story follows her through three decades of her life and her unrequited love for a boy whom she grows up with and has intermittent contact with over the years."

Or, keenly aware of the attention span of the average film executive, I could pitch it this way:

"It's *Forrest Gump*...but the main character is a girl instead of a boy."

What's the advantage of the second approach? It taps into something that already exists in the long-term memory of the

"The essence of persuasion has become the ability to fashion a compelling story."
—Daniel Pink

*Audiences already
know what a
"neighbor" is. There is
no need to explain it.*

film exec—*Forrest Gump*—and alters it. No work would be
required on the part of my audience to immediately understand
my concept.

Here are two more examples of tapping into concepts
that already exist in long-term memory to immediately convey
a point:

Everyone knows what dental floss is and what it does. The
brilliant team who created this Apple ad leveraged that
familiarity, altering the benefits of "flossing" to what an iMac can
do for your mind.

Or consider one of the oldest advertising campaigns in US
history, for State Farm insurance and its slogan: "Like a good
neighbor, State Farm is there." There's no work required on the
part of an audience to understand the concept of a "neighbor,"
which is exactly how the advertiser wants the public to think of
its brand.

EXERCISE

What is your CCO?

If you open your "Passion Trunk," what story or
experience can perfectly illustrate your CCO?

What story can you think of that comes from your
audience's collective experience?

IT DOESN'T GET ANY BETTER THAN THIS: SIMPLE, POWERFUL COMMUNICATION THAT LEVERAGES A CONCEPT THAT EXISTS IN OUR LONG-TERM MEMORY.

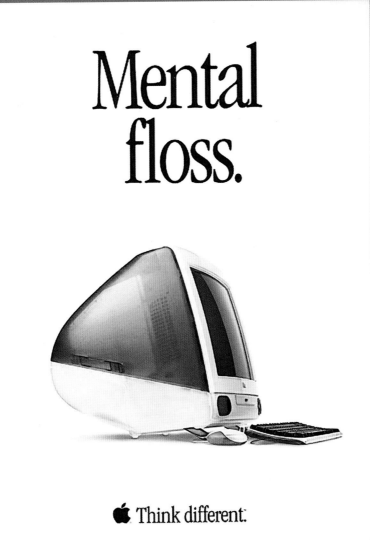

THE FIVE ESSENTIALS FOR YOUR TRIP

$$M = \frac{m_0}{\left(1 - \frac{v^2}{c^2}\right)^{1/2}} = \gamma m_0, \quad F = \frac{dp}{dt} = \frac{d}{dt}(Mv) = \frac{d}{dt}(\gamma m_0 v) = m_0 \frac{d}{dt}(\gamma v) = m_0 \left[\gamma \frac{dv}{dt} + v \frac{d\gamma}{dt}\right]$$

$$\frac{d\gamma}{dt} = \frac{d\gamma}{dv} \cdot \frac{dv}{dt} = \frac{d\gamma}{dv} \cdot a, \quad \frac{d\gamma}{dv} = \frac{d}{dv}\left(\frac{1}{\left(1 - \frac{v^2}{c^2}\right)^{1/2}}\right) = \underbrace{\frac{d\gamma}{d\beta} \cdot \frac{d\beta}{dv}}_{} \text{ where } \beta = \frac{v}{c}, \quad \frac{d\gamma}{d\beta} = \frac{d}{d\beta}\left(\frac{1}{(1-\beta^2)^{1/2}}\right)$$

$$= -\frac{1}{2}(-2\beta)(1-\beta^2)^{-3/2}$$

$$\Rightarrow \frac{d\gamma}{dv} = \frac{\beta(1-\beta^2)^{-3/2}}{c} = \frac{v}{c^2}\left(1 - \frac{v^2}{c^2}\right)^{-3/2} \qquad \frac{d\beta}{dv} = \frac{d}{dv}\left(\frac{v}{c}\right) \qquad = \beta(1-\beta^2)^{-3/2}$$

$$= \frac{1}{c}$$

$$\therefore F = m_0\left[\gamma \frac{dv}{dt} + v \frac{d\gamma}{dt}\right] = m_0\left[\gamma \frac{dv}{dt} + \frac{v}{c^2}\left(1 - \frac{v^2}{c^2}\right)^{-3/2} \cdot a\right] = m_0\left[\gamma a + \frac{v^2}{c^2}\left(1 - \frac{v^2}{c^2}\right)^{-3/2} \cdot a\right]$$

$$= m_0 a\left[\frac{1}{\left(1 - \frac{v^2}{c^2}\right)^{1/2}} + \frac{v^2}{c^2} \cdot \frac{1}{\left(1 - \frac{v^2}{c^2}\right)^{3/2}}\right], \quad \sigma = 1 - \frac{v^2}{c^2} \Rightarrow F = m_0 a\left[\frac{1}{\sigma^{1/2}} + \frac{v^2}{c^2} \cdot \frac{1}{\sigma^{3/2}}\right] = m_0 a\left[\frac{1}{\sigma^{1/2}} + \frac{(1-\sigma)}{\sigma^{3/2}}\right] = m_0 a\left[\frac{1}{\sigma^{3/2}}\right]$$

$$\therefore F = m_0 a\left[\frac{1}{\left(1 - \frac{v^2}{c^2}\right)^{3/2}}\right], \quad W = \int F \, dx = \int \frac{m_0 a}{\left(1 - \frac{v^2}{c^2}\right)^{3/2}} \, dx = m_0 \int \frac{1}{\left(1 - \frac{v^2}{c^2}\right)^{3/2}} \cdot \frac{dv}{dt} \, dx = m_0 \int \frac{v}{\left(1 - \frac{v^2}{c^2}\right)^{3/2}} \, dv$$

$$u = 1 - \frac{v^2}{c^2} \Rightarrow W = m_0\left[\frac{c^2}{-2}\int \frac{du}{u^{3/2}}\right] = m_0\left[\frac{-c^2}{2}\left[\frac{-u^{-1/2}}{-1/2}\right]\right] = m_0\left[\frac{c^2}{u^{1/2}}\right] = m_0\left[\frac{c^2}{\left(1 - \frac{v^2}{c^2}\right)^{1/2}}\right] + C$$

$$W = 0 \Rightarrow v = 0 \Rightarrow C = -m_0 c^2, \qquad W = \frac{m_0 c^2}{\left(1 - \frac{v^2}{c^2}\right)^{1/2}} - m_0 c^2 \Rightarrow W + m_0 c^2 = \frac{m_0 c^2}{\left(1 - \frac{v^2}{c^2}\right)^{1/2}}$$

$$\text{Total Energy} = W + m_0 c^2 = M c^2$$

Moving → not ↑ moving

or $$\boxed{E = M c^2}$$

YOUR LOGIC FLOW SHOULD
FLOW FROM LEFT TO RIGHT, LIKE A
MATHEMATICAL EQUATION.

If you're going to drive your audience from point "A" to point "B," you'd better have a route to guide you. Logic Flow is your route. The main points of your slides should flow logically, left to right. Like a mathematical equation, there should be a reason why one slide leads into the next. The sequence is of the same magnitude of importance as it would be to a lawyer in a closing argument.

The number one sign of a weak presentation is that the slides fail to build upon each other. So what does Logic Flow look like?

Moving from left to right, each of the headings below would be the main point for individual slides. See how each heading builds on the previous one?

UV rays are very powerful.   They are directly linked to skin cancer.   Today's SPF products offer excellent protection.   But too many people still don't use them.   And incidents of skin cancer are rising.

Logic Flows are best built using an unsung technology: the index card. Index cards are the building blocks of a presentation and what inspired the invention of PowerPoint in the first place. *Until you have your presentation assembled in a neat stack of index cards, don't go anywhere near a computer. Resist the temptation.*

My brother-in-law is a forensic psychologist. His CCO was to convince prosecutors that they needed to expose suspects trying to avoid conviction by faking illnesses.

His slides have a clear Logic Flow designed to drive his audience from point "A" (reticent) to point "B" (cooperative).

What does it look like when slides *aren't* connected?

Point "A" is your audience's point of view on the subject when they come into the room. Point "B" is where you want them to be on the subject when they leave.

Take a look at the three slides below on the topic of healthcare costs in the United States. These slides could be presented in any order. They don't build to a conclusive point but merely bombard the audience with data.

Revise the headings, and the Logic Flow becomes obvious:

"The percent of US GDP Continues to Rise"

"And the US Nearly Leads in Per-capita Healthcare"

"But the US Population Isn't Living Longer"

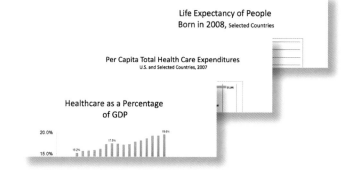

This author jumped the gun and started making his slides before he had the Logic Flow established. If we transcribe these original headings back to the index cards (where editing is easier and faster), we can see how they don't build on each other; no Logic Flow.

But the revised headings (caption, left) flow from point, to point, to point.

EXERCISE

Grab a stack of blank, ruled index cards. On the first index card write down your CCO. Then, on one index card at a time, write down each of your main points. Complete the first seven index cards, following your CCO card. Now play with the order of your cards. Mix them up. Which cards are essential, and which ones could be left out? See which Logic Flow is most effective.

What's
your CCO?

Main
point #1.

Main
point #2.

Main
point #3.

Main
point #4.

Main
point #5.

etc.

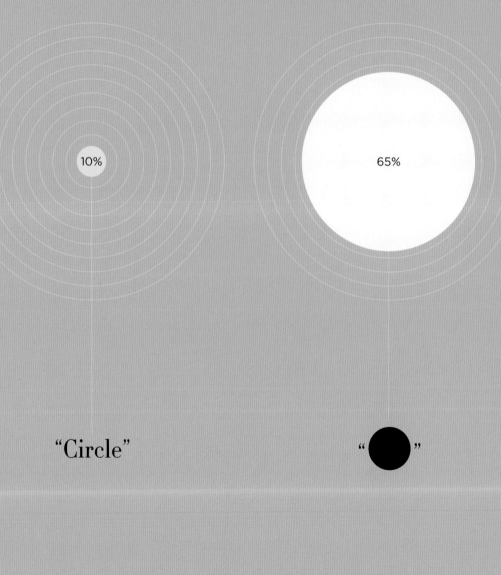

Who would go on a road trip without a camera? Likewise, who would create a whole presentation without utilizing images? Too many people. And I'm sure you've stifled yawns through more than your share of slide after slide of seemingly endless text.

The "Picture Superiority Effect" proves that concepts are more likely to be remembered if they're presented as pictures.

The slide on the left contains only text, headline, and main points. To the right, you see an image—intended to immediately communicate the meaning of the slide—along with a headline.

Who would create a presentation without utilizing images? Too many people.

In the slide on the right, an image has replaced the main points because the information contained in the main points will come from the speaker, the Master, who provides the caption for the image.

Which slide would you remember?

In another example, my client was making the point that her proposal to senior management was contradictory to company convention—so much so, that she felt like a heretic. To the left was her first choice for an image to illustrate that point (see figure on pg. 46). On the right is an alternate, more dramatic

An arsonist, a witch, and a businessman? How does this add up to "heretic"? The image on the far right works perfectly.

BILL PROUD

image to communicate the same thing. See the difference? Images add impact and immediacy, and they lead to better retention. *Choose your images wisely.* We may have survived the era of bad 1990's clip art, but you still need to select images with care and discretion. You want images that add depth and dimension to your point.

Many times a video clip can make a point more memorably than anything else, which is why major media companies like the *New York Times* are offering more video content on their sites than ever before.

If a particular clip from a movie, home video, commercial, or speech suits the purposes of your CCO, use it. YouTube is a fantastic resource for finding just about anything. There are several approaches to downloading video. I've found Keepvid.com to be easy and reliable.

How did my brother-in-law incorporate images into his presentation? He made initial scribblings of images that could be effective for each of his slides. But images for images' sake dilute the power of a presentation. You don't need to have one on every single slide to illustrate every single point. *Begin by finding an image or video clip that illustrates your CCO—then consider images for your other slides.*

MOON BUGGY OR $38 MILLION GOLF
CART? IT IS PICTURES LIKE THIS THAT
ARE TRULY WORTH A THOUSAND WORDS,
AND AUDIENCES DON'T FORGET THEM.

My brother-in-law decided to dispense with all but one: Pinocchio. We all know Pinocchio's nose grew when he told a lie, so using the illustration as a metaphor for suspects who lie about being ill communicates without any work required on the part of the audience. The audience has Pinocchio in their long-term memory, and they know what he was famous for.

THE PERFECT STORM

If your CCO is truly crystal clear, it's possible to find one image that perfectly captures it.

Consider my client's CCO for a presentation to his national sales team: to convince them that the media business has become completely unpredictable.

Snow in Jerusalem? Seeing is believing. The perfect image to communicate "unpredictability" to a sales force.

As it happened, a few days before the client was to deliver his presentation, a photo of snow in Jerusalem appeared on the front page of the *New York Times*. The story was about how weather patterns around the world have become so erratic and unpredictable that it actually snowed in the most unlikely place on earth: Jerusalem.

The photo so perfectly fit his objective that he used it as his first slide; no text, just the indelible image. He explained that just as global weather has become unpredictable, so has the media business. Sales forces need to prepare for new extremes if they are going to succeed.

GUIDELINES FOR SEARCHING AND SELECTING IMAGES OR VIDEO

Find an image or a video clip that illustrates your story.

Consider the sensibility of your audience so you don't run the risk of offending or alienating them.

Keepvid.com makes it easy to transfer video from YouTube to your PC or Mac. Google is a treasure trove of images (providing you get permission to use them); add "png" to the end of your search words and you will get "transparent" images without any background.

If you don't find an image that truly represents what you're looking for, keep searching. You'll be glad you did when you find exactly what you're looking for, and so will your audience.

In Google Images or Videos, a different or rearranged set of words will yield different results. Vary, change, and rearrange your search words if you don't find what you are looking for the first time.

Avoid obvious images that don't add depth to your point:

"We face a tough challenge." (picture of man pushing rock uphill)

"We must work together." (picture of business people holding hands)

"The rewards will be big." (picture of pot of gold at end of rainbow)

Be selective. Be spare. Be unexpected. Be original.

DON'T FORGET TO GET PERMISSION

Contrary to popular belief, not everything on the Internet, especially YouTube, is free for the taking. Before you copy and paste that perfect photo that will complement your presentation, verify its copyright status and review the terms of service on the website where you located the image. Even if the site claims that images are free or free with attribution, use may not be risk free. Videos are also copyrighted by the creator, and you need permission to use the video in your work.

Many images are published online under Creative Commons licenses, which may be used for presentations in many situations, including presentations for commercial purposes in some cases. Sites like Flickr and Google Images allow you to limit search results by specific license rights. Make sure you read the license terms to ensure you can use the image the way you want to use it.

Be careful—with one hasty click of your mouse, you could be downloading material without permission.

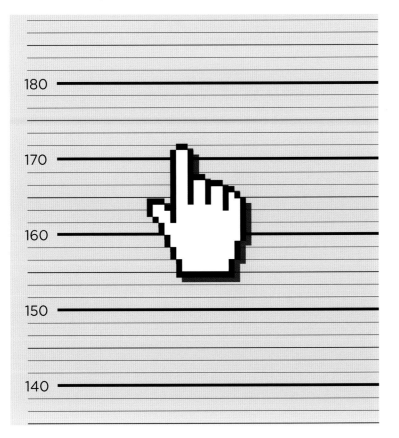

"One day, up in Heaven, God said to the men, 'I want you to form two lines.

'One line is for the men who are the head of the house.

'And the other line is for the men who let the woman be the head of the house.'

The line where the woman ran the house was a hundred miles long.

There was only one man in the other line.

God said, 'Men, I'm ashamed of you. I created you to be the head. Only one man stood up to make me proud.'

God turned to him and said, 'Son, tell 'em... how did you manage to be the only one in this line?'

The man looked kind of confused and said, 'I don't know. My wife told me to stand here.'"

Humor makes road trips go faster. It makes them memorable. And it can mean the difference between what an audience remembers and what they don't.

"[Humor] reduces hostility, deflects criticism, relieves tension, improves morale, and helps communicate difficult messages."
—Daniel Pink

Remind yourself what it's like to laugh out loud: search YouTube for *I Love Lucy* and Lucy's famous chocolate scene. It's as hilarious now as it ever was. There are lots of theories about the benefits of laughter. As a presenter, humor is invaluable because it allows you to engage and connect with your audience. And if the story or joke you're sharing is directly connected to your message, all the better.

A young televangelist makes a habit of starting off each program using humor: "I like to get started each week with something kinda funny." He makes an entire stadium of people laugh out loud as a way of getting them relaxed and ready to focus on his message. His story on the left is a favorite of mine.

With one funny story, the mood of an entire stadium can change. People become more relaxed and comfortable than when they'd walked in. And there is an enhanced sense of connection and intimacy between the speaker and his audience. You can have that same effect on an audience with humor. Try it and see for yourself.

SIMPLE GUIDELINES FOR USING HUMOR

If you're uncomfortable with or uncertain about humor, don't attempt it yourself. Let an image, quote, or video clip do it for you.

Don't try to impersonate someone else. Your sense of humor is yours. Never tell someone else's stories or jokes.

"The most effective executives deployed humor twice as often as middle-of-the-pack managers."
—Daniel Pink

LIKE A BOLT OF LIGHTNING, A LITTLE BIT OF CHARM AND HUMOR CAN INSTANTLY CHANGE THE MOOD OF AN ENTIRE STADIUM OF PEOPLE FOR THE BETTER.

The IBM Roadrunner
can process more
than one quadrillion
calculations per second."

vs

If all six billion people
on earth used hand
calculators and performed
calculations 24 hours
a day and seven days a week,
it would take them 46
years to do what the
Roadrunner can in one day."

What glove compartment would be complete without a flashlight? It's invaluable for retrieving bags from a dark trunk, coins from between seats, or keys from under them.

When you're speaking, your "flashlight" is used to ensure that a point will be unforgettable. Illumination magnifies a key point by putting it into context so that an audience can understand its magnitude or relevance immediately.

On the left is a sentence from an article written by a *New York Times* reporter to describe a new computer. But can people understand or relate to "one quadrillion" of anything?

In the same article, the reporter wrote the sentence, "If all six billion people on earth..."

Which description makes the most impact? Which one will his readers remember?

In the public service ad on the right, the advertiser is drawing attention to the gruesome statistics on teenage fatalities in automobile accidents. We can guess that their CCO was something like this: to convince the American public that the annual number of teenage deaths in car accidents is unacceptable.

"If 12 fully loaded jumbo jets crashed every year, something would be done about it. (Every year, more than 4,000 teens die in car crashes.)"

The advertiser employs the power of the headline and an illustration to illuminate its point for the reader. It wants to shock the public into paying attention.

Illumination puts a key point into context so that an audience can understand its magnitude or relevance immediately.

Here are some examples of the difference between merely stating a fact and illuminating one:

Fact: They spent $150 million on the project.

Illumination: They spent more on this one project than all 2012 projects combined.

Fact: For only $3 per month, you can provide food for an orphaned child.

Illumination: For the cost of a Big Mac, you can provide food for an orphaned child for a month.

Fact: The BP oil spill released 20,000 barrels of crude oil into the Gulf Coast.

Illumination: The BP oil spill released enough oil into the gulf coast to fill the entire Empire State Building.

EXERCISE

With your CCO in mind, pick one or two key points that are essential to building your argument and illuminate them.

Remember, you're trying to take a critical bit of information—a number, a fact, a statistic—and make it unforgettable.

Put it into context, and your audience won't forget it.

EVEN IF THE *WASHINGTON POST* LOST $100 MILLION A YEAR, JEFF BEZOS'S PERSONAL FORTUNE COULD FUND IT FOR 252 YEARS.

ington Po

"I HAVE A DREAM...
I HAVE A DREAM...
I HAVE A DREAM...
I HAVE A DREAM...
I HAVE A DREAM...
I HAVE A DREAM...
I HAVE A DREAM...
I HAVE A DREAM...
I HAVE A DREAM."

Many presenters think that if they've made an important point once, it's been made.

But if it starts to rain during your road trip, just one swipe of the windshield wipers doesn't enable you to see clearly. It's the repeating wipe, wipe, wipe that allows you to navigate during the storm.

Likewise, great speakers know the value of repeating a point, especially when it's the main thrust of their argument. Take Martin Luther King Jr.'s famous speech delivered on the mall in Washington, DC, in 1963. Even though he delivered it over 50 years ago, people still remember one key phrase: "I have a dream."

Why?

Because Dr. King repeated the phrase a second, third, and a total of nine times. *Nine times.* It was the centerpiece of his speech, and he knew that through repetition the crowd of over 200 thousand people, and the rest of the world watching, would remember it. He was right.

In President Obama's inaugural address, on the issue of gun control he repeated, "They deserve a vote" over and over to make the point that Congress should take up the issue and put it to a vote.

"Gabby Giffords deserves a vote."

"The families of Newtown deserve a vote."

"The families of Aurora deserve a vote."

Martin Luther King Jr. repeated "I have a dream" nine times, making sure people remembered it—50 years later.

Want people to remember a key point? Open with it; repeat it midway through your presentation; and close with it. Do that and they will remember.

In the movie *Dog Day Afternoon*, Al Pacino shouts "Attica" over 15 times to make sure the crowd remembered the Attica prison riot that left 29 prisoners dead.

If you want people to remember a key point, fact, quote, or statistic, make sure you repeat it a second or even third time. Do it and your audience won't forget.

EXERCISE

What one key point do you want to make sure your audience remembers?

Look for the organic, dramatic moments in your presentation where you can repeat it.

Find a way to repeat it to your audience three times.

I HAVE A DREAM

IF YOU HAVE SOMETHING YOU WANT
PEOPLE TO REMEMBER, BE SURE TO TELL
THEM MORE THAN ONCE.

DON'T ASK YOUR AUDIENCE TO READ SOMETHING WHILE YOU'RE TALKING TO THEM

THE SPLIT-ATTENTION EFFECT:
WHEN WHAT YOU SAY COMPETES WITH
WHAT YOU SHOW AN AUDIENCE.

If you present a slide full of text and then begin speaking to your audience, you are making them choose between you and your slides. *Don't.*

All too often there's no obvious connection between the information on a slide and what the presenter says while presenting it.

Most people don't realize that the human brain processes visual and audio input via the same channel: a single-lane highway bringing pictures and sounds to our brains.

When speech and visuals don't reinforce each other, but compete for our attention, the audience is forced to choose. Like a baby distracted by a shiny object, the audience's attention will always go to the slide (shiny object) first and then to the speaker. This phenomenon is called the "Split-Attention Effect."

So how do you avoid this all-too-common mistake?

1. Keep it simple.

A good slide is like a billboard; the audience should be able to read it as if they were driving by at 65 miles per hour. That means they can absorb a slide in less than 10 seconds, then return their attention to you.

2. Ensure correlation.

Make sure there is obvious correlation between what you're saying and what you're showing. You want listening to be effortless for the audience, with slides that complement and emphasize what you are saying.

MYTH: "I don't need to worry if what I say doesn't match my slide."

REALITY: People understand a presentation better when they don't split their attention between competing sources of information.

BREAK UP YOUR TRIP TO KEEP YOUR AUDIENCE'S ATTENTION

THREE THINGS YOU SHOULD DO IN EVERY PRESENTATION: SLOW DOWN (BUILD), PULL OVER TO REST AREA (PAUSE), HONK (HIGHLIGHT)

Would you sign up for a nonstop trip, without opportunities to take in the important sights? This is not a sprint. If you don't slow down, pause, and highlight key things along the way, you risk losing your audience's attention—and never getting it back.

In every presentation be sure to

> slow down (*Build*);
>
> pull over to rest area (*Pause*);
>
> sound your horn (*Highlight*).

THE BUILD

This one simple thing, if properly applied, could improve the impact of presentations the world over. This is the process whereby one word, phrase, object, or image appears on your slide and then, when you're finished elaborating on it, you click and move on to the next.

Rather than a whole slide of information appearing at once, the elements appear successively—in a "build"—so that the audience can absorb each section, one section at a time. A build makes it easy for an audience to follow along and absorb what you're presenting.

Just remember: what's on the slide is meant to be the short headline—not complete sentences or paragraphs. You are the one providing the "caption" for each slide.

Your job is to break up the trip and vary the tempo to make sure the audience's attention stays on you.

THE PAUSE

In a presentation about how "I love music," a pause slide allows speakers to tell a humorous story about an embarrassing experience they had in eighth-grade dance class, an experience that has kept them from dancing in public ever since. Or ask how many people in the audience like to dance. What kind of dance? Ballroom? Salsa? Hip-hop?

A pause in the stream of the presentation allows you to vary your pace, check in with your audience, and make sure they're awake and engaged. It changes the rhythm of your presentation and increases your chances of retaining their attention.

THE HIGHLIGHT

This is all about drawing attention to certain points on your slides and adding emphasis. It can be done with boldface type, a different color type, an image, or a video clip.

In this example, presenters might want to share the reason why they don't dance hip-hop—using video to bring the point to life with a little humor.

The video clip on the left is of traditional ballroom dancing, which a presenter learned in eighth grade and is comfortable with. The video clip on the right is of hip-hop dancing, demonstrating the skill and courage required to do it well; the same skill and courage the presenter doesn't possess.

Why not use video clips to highlight your point?

In this grave hour, perhaps the most fateful in our history, I send to every household of my peoples, both at home and overseas, this message. Spoken with the same depth of feeling for each one of you as if I were able to cross your threshold and speak to you myself.

For the second time in the lives of most of us, we are at war!

Over and over again, we have tried to find a peaceful way out of the differences between ourselves and those who are now our enemies; but it has been in vain.

We have been forced into a conflict, for we are called, with our allies, to meet the challenge of a principle which, if it were to prevail, would be fatal to any civilized order in the world.

in this grave hour perhaps the most fateful in our history I send to every household of my peoples both at home and overseas this message spoken with the same depth of feeling for each one of you as if I were able to cross your threshold and speak to you myself for the second time in the lives of most of us we are at war over and over again we have tried to find a peaceful way out of the differences between ourselves and those who are now our enemies but it has been in vain we have been forced into a conflict for we are called with our allies to meet the challenge of a princi-ple which if it were to prevail would be fatal to any civilized order in the world

EVEN KINGS KNOW HOW VITAL IT IS TO ADD PACING AND VARY TEMPO. THIS SPEECH, FROM KING GEORGE VI, WAS THE MOST IMPORTANT ONE OF HIS LIFE. DO YOU THINK IT WOULD HAVE HAD THE SAME IMPACT IF IT WAS JUST ONE LONG RUN-ON SENTENCE?

ONLY PACK THE ESSENTIALS

ONLY THE HEADLINES,
THE TIP OF THE
ICEBERG, APPEAR
ON YOUR SLIDES;
YOU PROVIDE ALL THE
DETAIL TO ILLUSTRATE
YOUR POINTS.

SLIDE

SPEAKER

In great presentations, the slides contain just the tip of the iceberg, the key points. What's below the surface of the water—the detail—comes from the speaker. If you overload your slides with nonessential information, you risk losing your audience in record time.

How do you determine which information is vital? Ask yourself: Would my Logic Flow work without this piece of information? If it does, then it's nonessential.

In order to create slides that support rather than replace you, it's necessary to extract the key information from each.

Fired or laid off, joining the unemployed does not feel good.

Job loss may indeed trigger serious physiological illness.

80% of unemployed workers are diagnosed with a new health problem 18 months later.

Blue-collar workers were harder hit by job loss, both physically and mentally.

Anxiety can make us vulnerable to stroke, hypertension, and heart disease.

The trick is to keep the slide (above) simple by putting the speaking points in "Presenter's Notes" (below), where they belong.

Media/Budget Planning Parameters

- 2010 – A "reset" year
  - Product and communication evolved to ensure they resonate with consumers
  - New product and communication approach needs to be supported to ensure adequate awareness and understanding levels to build this brand and deliver against expectations
- Budget priorities
  - Reach and frequency critical to build awareness and ensure both old and new customers are drawn to the brand
  - Continuity is needed to ensure frequency goals are met and consumers keep the brand top of mind in a highly cluttered and advertising intensive retail category
    - Increased TV continuity critical to build awareness and remain top of mind during key shopping periods. Consider 6-8 week Cable plan with 3-4 week Primetime Broadcast heavy-up
    - Minimum 6 months of Print in core, targeted titles, utilizing a combination of ROB Spreads and Pages plus multi-page inserts
    - On-line continuity is essential to both build awareness and increase click-thru to website
  - Advertising Communications Goal:
    - 75% Reach/4.0 Frequency average 4-week/month
  - Consistent presence in pre-prints to drive frequency amongst key shoppers

Media/Budget Planning Parameters

- 2010 – A "reset" year
  - Product and communication evolved to ensure they resonate with consumers
  - New product and communication approach needs to be supported to ensure adequate awareness and understanding levels to build this brand and deliver against expectations
- Budget priorities
  - Reach and frequency critical to build awareness and ensure both old and new customers are drawn to the brand
  - Continuity is needed to ensure frequency goals are met and consumers keep the brand top of mind in a highly cluttered and advertising intensive retail category
    - Increased TV continuity critical to build awareness and remain top of mind during key shopping periods. Consider 6-8 week Cable plan with 3-4 week Primetime Broadcast heavy-up
    - Minimum 6 months of Print in core, targeted titles, utilizing a combination of ROB Spreads and Pages plus multi-page inserts
    - On-line continuity is essential to both build awareness and increase click-thru to website
  - Advertising Communications Goal:
    - 75% Reach/4.0 Frequency average 4-week/month
  - Consistent presence in pre-prints to drive frequency amongst key shoppers

Media/Budget Planning Parameters

- 2010 – A "reset" year
  - Product and communication evolved
  - Needs to be supported
- Budget priorities
  - Reach and frequency critical
  - Continuity is needed
    - TV
    - Print
    - On-line

1. Here's the original slide.

I doubt there's much information about this topic that has not been included on this slide. But it's a slide, not a page from a textbook. These facts are meant to be the talking points, not read by the audience or (worse) the presenter.

2. Here's the essential information circled in red.

These are the headlines; the key points that the presenter needs to cover. They represent the essential information without which your slide doesn't make the points it's supposed to.

3. Here's the updated slide.

Imagine each of these main points appearing *sequentially*, and you can imagine how a presenter would present this slide:

Click to the first key point.

Provide the detail for that point.

Click to the next key point, etc.

So where does the information belong that you just extracted? In the appendix or leave-behind. That is what they were made for.

TECHNOLOGY SLIDE

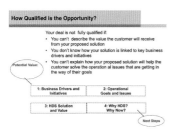

Here's another example of a slide that reads like a page from a book. Is the presenter going to read every word aloud? Is the audience expected to attempt to read every word before the presenter clicks to the next slide?

And here's the simplified version, with the nonessential information extracted, to be delivered one point at a time, so the focus remains on the speaker.

Overburdened slides are typically the result of decks being circulated for approval by various individuals within an organization, who pile details on every slide.

Print your slides in "Speaker's Notes" format, so that anyone reviewing the deck can see the actual slide along with the speaker's notes. These notes communicate exactly what you intend to cover on each slide. Reviewers can then confine their edits or comments to the "Speaker's Notes" area, keeping your slides from being overloaded.

To ensure your slides only contain essential information:

Print out your existing slides, one, three, or six slides per page.

Circle all essential information/key points on each slide.

Create new index cards:

Transfer the headings to the cards.

Transfer the essential information to the cards as key points, below the heading, one by one.

Try to limit yourself to three key points per slide.

This is what a slide that is overloaded with text looks (and feels) like to an audience.

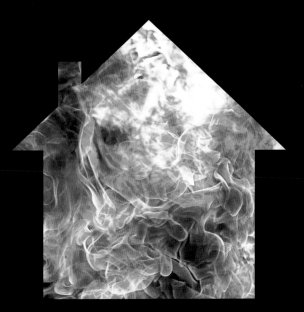

ELABORATE FORMATTING, DROP SHADOWS, OUTLINES, AND COLORS MAKE IT HARDER FOR YOUR AUDIENCE TO UNCOVER YOUR POINTS. MAKE IT EASY BY KEEPING ANY GRAPHS, TABLES, OR CHARTS SIMPLE AND CLEAN.

DON'T MAKE YOUR AUDIENCE DIG THROUGH
YOUR SLIDES TO FIND WHAT'S IMPORTANT

When it comes to slides that communicate clearly and immediately, less is more. An audience should be able to grasp a slide in 10 seconds or less—as if it were a billboard they were driving by at 65 miles per hour.

And yet too many presenters still clutter their slides with unnecessary visual noise that makes the audience work too hard to uncover their meaning. Bullet points are the most pervasive offender—they add nothing and actually distract attention. *Don't use them.* A simple indentation and double spacing will do a more effective job of highlighting your points.

When it comes to tables, charts, and graphs, it is even more important to be spare. If your audience is going to grasp the meaning of data—year-over-year sales, relative crop yields, growth trends—you must present it clearly and simply. Today's presentation software offers a multitude of options for creating 3-D tables and charts, but these complex visuals obscure your data and actually make it harder for your audience to understand.

Bullet points are a relic of the past and only distract from the content of the points you are trying to make. Don't use them. Let your key points speak for themselves.

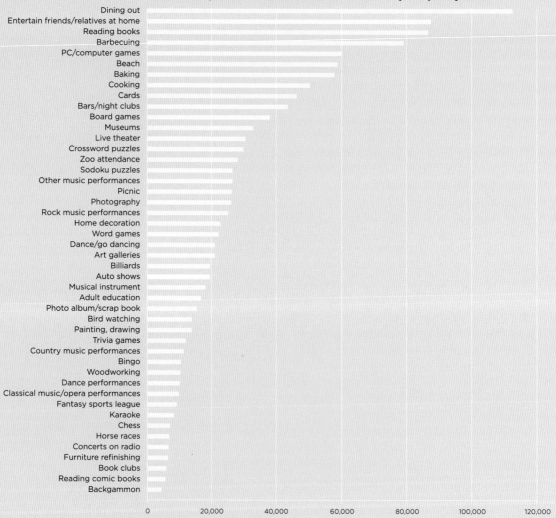

Adult Participation in Selected Leisure Activities by Frequency: 2010

Dining out
Entertain friends/relatives at home
Reading books
Barbecuing
PC/computer games
Beach
Baking
Cooking
Cards
Bars/night clubs
Board games
Museums
Live theater
Crossword puzzles
Zoo attendance
Sodoku puzzles
Other music performances
Picnic
Photography
Rock music performances
Home decoration
Word games
Dance/go dancing
Art galleries
Billiards
Auto shows
Musical instrument
Adult education
Photo album/scrap book
Bird watching
Painting, drawing
Trivia games
Country music performances
Bingo
Woodworking
Dance performances
Classical music/opera performances
Fantasy sports league
Karaoke
Chess
Horse races
Concerts on radio
Furniture refinishing
Book clubs
Reading comic books
Backgammon

0   20,000   40,000   60,000   80,000   100,000   120,000

**ANY GRAPH OR CHART SHOULD COMMUNICATE
YOUR POINT CLEARLY AND IMMEDIATELY; THE RELATIONSHIP
BETWEEN THE DATA SHOULD BE OBVIOUS.**
(You shouldn't need to be a statistician to figure out which
number is the biggest and which is the smallest.)

DO THESE

Use data labels vs. legends.

Use only one warm color per data set, including pie charts.

Highlight specific data with a different shade
vs. a different color (see left).

Sort horizontal bar charts in the order of the data.

Spell out names, months (January, February, March).

Use four-digit years when feasible or 2001, 02, 03.

DON'T DO THESE

Use bright contrasting colors.

Use 3-D effects.

Add shading or shadows.

Use angled text.

Use more than five slices in a pie chart.

Use special effects (shading, pull-out slices) for pie charts.

Use two-character abbreviations for states.

TYPOGRAPHY TIPS

Avoid self-conscious, hard-to-read fonts; Helvetica or
Garamond are always good and modern choices.

Use up to 80 point for headlines.

Don't use smaller than 30 point for any type, on any slide.

*"Admit colors into
charts gracefully,
as you would
receive in-laws
into your home."*
—Dona Wong

PUT EVERYTHING IN PLACE BEFORE YOU START

Disciplined chefs have everything they need to prepare a dish ready to go before they begin. They call it *mise en place*, which means "everything in place." But if you're like me, your instinct is to bypass this step, jump right in, and take the "prepare as you go" approach.

"Mise en place" means that you have done all the preparation work ahead of time; everything you need is right in front of you.

Resist the temptation to skip your presentation prep work, and when the time comes to transfer everything to your PowerPoint slides, it will be the quickest and easiest part of your process. If you start assembling a presentation in PowerPoint before you've completed your index cards and established a clear Logic Flow, you're putting the cart before the horse. It is much faster and easier to create, edit, arrange, and rearrange index cards until you get it right.

Remember, index cards were the precursor and the inspiration for PowerPoint. *Use them.*

If you haven't already done it, write your CCO
as a phrase that begins with "to convince."

Then:

Write a heading for each slide on separate index cards.

Arrange your cards in the best Logic Flow.

Write one to three key points to support
the main point of each heading.

Write all notations for images, humor, repetition, illumination.

Create one or two pause slides.

Create a final card that reconnects the audience back
to your first slide, your story.

*Make sure that 95
percent of your
thinking and 100
percent of your
index cards are
complete before
you go anywhere
near a computer, or
you'll regret it.*

STAY CONNECTED AND YOU'LL GET THERE

THE UNIVERSE OF PRESENTATIONS
CONSISTS OF ONLY THREE THINGS:
YOU, YOUR CONTENT, AND YOUR
AUDIENCE. YOUR JOB IS TO ALWAYS BE
CONNECTING TO TWO OF THEM:
YOUR CONTENT AND YOUR AUDIENCE.

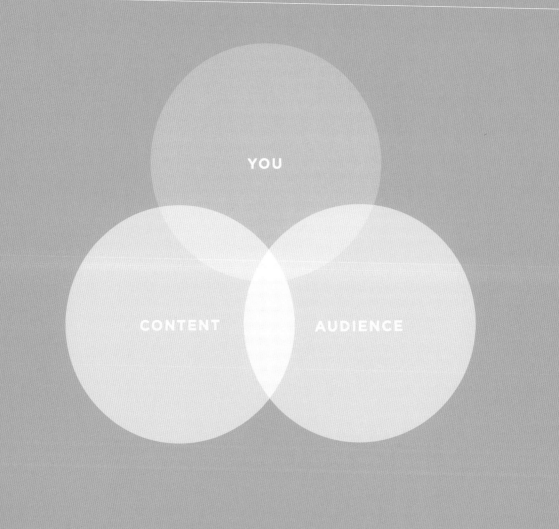

You can do all of this work to create the perfect, most compelling presentation, but if you're not connected to your content and your audience, it's doomed.

If this is a work presentation, it's helpful to keep in mind that connecting to your content is not elective. You're being paid to convince that audience of something. So before you give your next presentation, ask yourself three questions:

What is at stake for me?

Who will this presentation affect?

Why do I care about it?

You must be able to answer all three of these questions, even if your only answer is that you care about it because you want to keep your job or cover you mortgage. *Find your motivation.*

Connection means the difference between a presenter who is "phoning it in" and a presenter who's actively engaged with the audience every minute of the presentation.

Here's how it works:

If you're not connected to your content and your audience, your presentation is doomed.

YOUR CONTENT

To be truly connected to what you're saying and to be in a position to convince an audience of something, you have to be fluent in the topic.

If you love biking or bowling or cooking or World War II history, you read about it, spend free time on it, and get pleasure out of it. Just like with personal experiences, the phenomenon about passions is that you can talk about them comfortably and at length—because you know them and love them.

I'VE NEVER MET A CLIENT WHO
DIDN'T LAUNCH INTO A TOTALLY
CONNECTED MONOLOGUE
WHEN I ASKED THEM ABOUT
ONE OF THEIR PASSIONS.

What's your favorite restaurant?

What is your favorite sports team?

What was your best vacation?

I've never met a client who didn't launch into a totally connected monologue when I asked about a passion:

No hesitation.

No rehearsal.

No nervousness.

The trick is to maintain that same level of connection when you're presenting for work. The subject has changed, but your level of passion has to remain the same if you're going to convince an audience of anything.

When I find clients slipping into monotone, disinterested in their own presentation and sounding like a bored flight attendant reciting "if the cabin pressure should change…," I stop them. I ask them to talk about one of their passions, to restore an authentic connection and animation for a topic. Then I start them again with their work presentation.

Golden idol or bag of sand—Indiana Jones's life hung in the balance—and your job is to maintain the same intensity and awareness of the stakes no matter what you are presenting: your favorite vacation or quarterly sales results.

YOUR AUDIENCE

Okay, you care. *Now act like it.*

If you want to connect with an audience, you must do so one person at a time. But you will never hear me talk about "eye contact" because it sounds (and looks) mechanical and contrived.

The only reason to connect with your audience is to see how they're reacting to what you are saying:

Do they look angry?

Do they look confused?

Do they look unhappy?

Do they look bored?

Did they laugh at your story or joke?

If you aren't looking at them—right at their faces— how can you know?

Pretend that you cannot breathe unless you are looking into the faces of your audience 90 percent of the time.

In acting there is a technique called "as if" that's used to help students get an immediate understanding of a particular behavior, so they can demonstrate it convincingly. Imagine when presenting to an audience that it's "as if" you cannot breathe unless you're looking into the faces of the people in the room 90 percent of the time. It's a surefire way of staying connected to your audience.

But how do you simultaneously connect with both your audience and your slides?

Here's an industry secret: the best teacher is your weatherman. Turn on your local news.

Learn the art of connection from your weatherman

It doesn't matter which country or city, the local weatherman is universal. His hallmark is the ability to refer to his content (the green screen behind him) and relate to his audience (looking directly into the camera).

Great presenters do the same thing. They refer to their slides by pointing or gesturing and relate to their audience by looking them directly in their faces.

So can you. While you keep your main focus on your audience, you can refer to your slides with one hand (touch the screen if possible). You can also intermittently look at your slides, but stay 90 percent focused on your audience.

Bottom line: you should be referring to your content 10 percent and relating to your audience 90 percent of the time.

USE EVERY TOOL IN THE TRUNK

If you want to truly connect and convince an audience of something, use everything at your disposal. You may not be an actor, but you have the same tools.

To see an actor fully deploy all the tools in his instrument you need look no further than Marlon Brando's performance as

YOUR

voice quality

facial expressions

variations in wording

body movement

intonation

individual style

volume/speed of speech

body positions

mannerisms

Marc Antony in the movie *Julius Caesar*. He delivers one of Shakespeare's most memorable speeches at Caesar's funeral, which begins with the famous words: "Friends, Romans, countrymen...lend me your ears."

Marc Antony's CCO was to convince the crowd that Caesar was a good man—a crowd celebrating Caesar's assassination. His goal was to transport them from point "A" (hatred) to point "B" (love). Had Brando not fully utilized all the tools he had to draw from, his Marc Antony would have failed. But what was more important: What he said? Or how he said it?

Communication is more about HOW you say it than WHAT you say: your tone of voice and your body language. So you want to use them both to be convincing to your audience.

Effectiveness of Spoken Communication

content	
tone of voice	
body language	

0   10   20   30   40   50   60

A UCLA study concluded that 93 percent of effective spoken communication consists of only two things:

body language

tone of voice

That means what you say may not be as convincing or memorable to an audience as how you say it. So if you want to maximize your chances for success, use all your tools and stay connected.

And finally. . .

MARC ANTONY'S CRYSTAL CLEAR OBJECTIVE: TO CONVINCE THE MOB THAT CAESAR WAS A GOOD MAN.

WHEN YOU ADVANCE FROM SLIDE TO SLIDE, AND YOUR AUDIENCE HAS NO IDEA HOW YOU'RE DOING IT, IT SEEMS LIKE MAGIC...AND KEEPS ALL THEIR ATTENTION ON YOU.

NEVER LET THEM SEE YOU CLICK

Nothing makes you look more unsophisticated, unprofessional, and unrehearsed than conspicuous clicking to advance your slides. It is an unnecessary distraction.

Do you make a public announcement every time you turn the page when reading a newspaper or magazine?

So before any presentation, as part of your rehearsal, your job is to discover where you need to point when you click, and then click stealthily, "as if" you were doing it telepathically.

Great presenters are as subtle as a sphinx when they click from one point or one slide to the next, ensuring there are no distractions between them, their content, and their audience. *Practice and you will be able to do it too.*

Nothing makes you look more like an amateur than conspicuously clicking.

YOUR GPS FOR ANY ROAD TRIP

I HOPE TO SAVE YOU TIME AND WIN BUSINESS. HERE IS AN AT-A-GLANCE SUMMARY.

HEADLINE

Support point
Support point
Support point

BLANK SLIDE

The first slide for each of my clients is identical: it's blank—a moment of calm before beginning. It gives the audience the luxury of being able to focus solely on you. Welcome the audience, tell them a joke, ask them a question, tell them how much time of theirs you will be taking, and then [*CLICK*] to begin your presentation.

IMAGE / VIDEO SLIDE

The second slide is the story that communicates your CCO. It can be an image or a video clip that illustrates your CCO. Remember the supply-chain story? His first slide was a picture of a German Panzer tank. With just one image on the slide, he told his story about how a supply chain is critical, whether for WWII battles or retail stores.

LOGIC FLOW SLIDES

The main point of each of these slides is expressed in each brief headline. They should flow from point to point. You can also add images for impact—but curate cautiously, making sure each image adds depth and meaning to your point. *Don't use an image for every slide.* A few words centered on a slide can have just as much impact.

HEADLINE

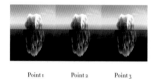

Point 1   Point 2   Point 3

PAUSE

NONTEMPLATE SLIDES

Rigid slide templates mute the impact of the content. Vary the layout and configuration of slides—it keeps the audience awake and allows for flexibility to tailor each slide according to its mission.

PAUSE SLIDES

These slides are your opportunity to stop, emphasize, and reel in the audience with a story or question—anything that will keep them engaged and focused. It mixes up the rhythm, keeps it from becoming boring, and lets you see how your audience is reacting.

FINAL SLIDE

Let this final slide bring the audience back to where you started: the Crystal Clear Objective that you illustrated with your story. It's a proven rhetorical technique called "bookending"; a form of repetition that increases the chances that your audience will remember your CCO.

**WHAT TO DO
AT-A-GLANCE:**

◉ What is your
Audience's Perspective?

◉ What is your
Crystal Clear Objective?

📖 Come up with a Story that
perfectly illustrates your CCO.

👣 Start your Logic Flow one
heading, one card at a time.

📷 Add in your
supporting visuals.

☺ Incorporate the
incredible power of humor.

✒ Illuminate: pick one or
two key points essential
to building your argument
and illuminate them.

🔦 Repeat: look for the moments
where you can repeat a key point.
And then create your last slide that
brings your audience back to where
you began – your opening story.

ABOUT THE AUTHOR

Nothing will accelerate your career faster than developing your ability to communicate.

Michael Baldwin is an accomplished leader in the communications industry, with more than 35 years of experience in building global brands, leading global teams, solving complex strategic problems, and developing world-class creative campaigns.

He is founder and CEO of MICHAEL BALDWIN INC, which offers best-in-class personal and corporate branding, executive and team coaching and development, and training that turns presenters into truly effective communicators. Simply put, Michael helps individuals, teams, companies, and brands be better.

Michael spent seven years with Ogilvy & Mather New York, where he was the worldwide account director for the IBM and SAP accounts, building integrated campaigns and global teams in over 40 countries.

He is a highly decorated creative professional, having won the David Ogilvy Award for his leadership on the SAP global brand campaign and Cannes Gold Lion, Clio, British D&AD Silver, and *AdAge's* "Best of the Year" TV campaign awards for copywriting.

Michael has held posts at other top agencies, such as Ammirati & Puris, BBDO, and FCB, where he managed accounts that included Apple, Compaq, Ashton-Tate and NeXT.

Michael has led executive coaching programs on leadership, team building, presentation skills, and maximizing personal impact for companies such as Credit Suisse, American Express, and Goldman Sachs.

He delivered nearly 1,000 iApps theater presentations at the flagship Apple Store in New York and is an official mentor to early-stage technology companies via the Entrepreneurs Roundtable Accelerator program and for The Funding Network.

His clients include Dow Jones, Forbes, NYU, Ogilvy & Mather, Initiative, Bloomberg, The New York Times, IPG Media Brands, Ralph Lauren, Universal McCann, and others.

Michael studied acting at the William Esper Studio and the Deena Levy Theatre Studio in New York. He has a BS from Beloit College and resides in New York.

For information about training programs and consulting services, visit baldwin.com

Just Add Water was made possible in part by the following people who preordered the book on Inkshares.com. Thank you.

Anne C Goulandris
Caroline L Von Stade
Charles Kemper
Claudia J Maupin
C Reynolds Parsons
Cristina Trujillo Lilly
David Baldwin
David Jackson
Ellen Schmitt
Frances v Downing
Harvey J Carroll
James M Woodhull, II
Jennifer A Siebens
Jennifer Williams
Jonathan axelrod
Keri Kay Taylor
L M Koning
L R Parsons
Mark A Rosen
Megan Kent
Meredith Kopit Levien
Murat Aktihanoglu
Susannah Baldwin
Thorsten Schulz
William F Peck

INKSHARES

Inkshares is a crowdfunded publisher. We democratize publishing by letting readers select the books we publish – we edit, design, print, distribute and market any book that meets a pre-order threshold.

Interested in making a book idea come to life? Visit inkshares.com to find new projects or start your own.

CREDITS

Catherine Johnson: Editor of photography and visual

Marc Klein: Creative direction and design. kleinmarc.com

Page 16	Part of an extensively annotated music sheet of Mozart's Fantasia in D minor. ©Andre Nantel. Licensed from Shutterstock
Page 20	©Cheney / The New Yorker Collection / www.cartoonbank.com
Page 29	©Licensed by The New York Times/Redux
Page 30	Gustave Doré's illustration of Jean de La Fontaine's fable *Le Singe et le Chat*, 1867 - Public Domain
Page 37	Billboard. ©Apple Inc.
Page 40	©Benmoat. Licensed by Shutterstock
Page 45	Diving image. ©Susannah Baldwin
Page 46	Witch cartoon. ©Bill Proud. Licensed from Cartoon Stock. Burning of witches by inquisition in a German marketplace. After a drawing by H. Grobert.©Bettmann/CORBIS
Page 48	NASA Apollo 17 Lunar Roving Vehicle, 11 December 1972—Public Domain image created by NASA
Page 53	UNITED STATES—CIRCA 2012: a postage stamp printed in USA commemorative of the american television program *I Love Lucy*, Circa 2012.©Catwalker. Licensed by Shutterstock
Page 57	Ad. ©Allstate
Page 60	Licensed by Writers House LLC. Reprinted by arrangement with The Heirs to the Estate of Martin Luther King Jr., c/o Writers House as agent for the proprietor New York, NY
Page 84	Chart source: GfK MRI
Page 95	*Indiana Jones and the Raiders of the Lost Ark*, 1981. ©Lucas Film Ltd./Paramount. The Kobal Collection
Page 98	A televised weather report for the British Isles. ©Hulton-Deutsch Collection/CORBIS
Page 101	Marlon Brando on the set of *Julius Caesar*, based on the play by William Shakespeare and directed by Joseph L. Mankiewicz, 1953. ©Metro-Goldwyn-Mayer Pictures/Sunset Boulevard/Corbis

Art and icon art ©Marc Klein: pages 9, 34, 44, 51, 66, 70, 77, 89, 93, 94, 100, and 103.

All other images are copyrighted and licensed by Shutterstock.

JUST ADD WATER is a registered trademark of MICHAEL BALDWIN INC.